Life in between

Life in between

A Collection of Poems and Photographs

Maria Pisciotta-DellaPorte

LIFE IN BETWEEN
A COLLECTION OF POEMS AND PHOTOGRAPHS

iUniverse books may be ordered through booksellers or by contacting:

iUniverse
1663 Liberty Drive
Bloomington, IN 47403
www.iuniverse.com
1-800-Authors (1-800-288-4677)

ISBN: 978-1-5320-0214-4 (sc)
ISBN: 978-1-4917-9048-9 (e)

Library of Congress Control Number: 2016903625

Print information available on the last page.

iUniverse rev. date: 07/25/2016

To my daughter, Laura Marilyn—

The first time your voice was revealed to me, crying out, I fell in love. Our eyes met, and an instant silence came over you. You looked at me intently then were content. You knew I was your mother; the body holding you safely all along, and you had been waiting to meet me. I took you in my arms with complete joy. My desire in that instance and in every moment after was to make the world and life perfect for you. As we all know, it is an impossible task, but we strive for the best.

I have countless memories in my heart of your smiles, playfulness, laughter, tears, dancing, achievements, and celebrations … of our times together reading, taking walks, playing, baking, dressing up, talking, planning … of your birthdays, Christmas, swimming, colds and tummy aches, camp, vacations. We are mother and daughter by the gift of God and friends through the way of our hearts.

My wish for you is to learn as much as you can, to see many beautiful things in the world, to love with all your heart, to forgive, to be at peace, to have faith, to learn from your mistakes, to command respect, to be loved completely, to be charitable, to laugh, laugh, laugh, and to feel safe when you cry. And I hope times of sorrow are few and times of joy are many.

Make your life rich with all that counts. Know your heart; know mine too and that it is always with you.

I love you, always, forever.
Mom

CONTENTS

ACKNOWLEDGMENTS

A special thank-you to Ariel Williams, the photographer on this project. I am proud to have your work included as a special part of this book and grateful to you personally for your beautiful creativity. Thank you for your insight, consideration, sensitivity, and connection to my work. Thank you for your input and for making our collaboration an absolute pleasure. I am happy to have met you. Here's to all your future creative successes!

Ariel I. Williams is a fine art photographer born in 1993 and currently lives on Long Island, NY. Her BFA in Photography was received from New York City's Fashion Institute of Technology in 2015. By disposition more of an observer than a participant, or being a combiner-of-symbols, she reflects and unearths inner states in the external. These visual notes are a memoir through record at the same time being a play with imaginative narration.

INTRODUCTION

I found myself gasping for time. It was being pulled out from my solar plexus, comparable to giving birth. I felt as if my soul were violently departing, converting me into someone I was yet to know. Then abruptly, as if I swallowed the world, it stopped. Every joy and sorrow became a compilation reverberating inside of me. My eyes opened. All I could see at first were my own pupils—too tiny. When light began to shine in, awareness was painful. I watched from within as they dilated, and an intelligence, a force, bonded with me and simultaneously separated. With each expanding, I saw my own face like a map. Each hard line, each pale brown spot, each enlarged pore—all connected to some story: a memory, a person, hope, sorrow, past, myself, and a life that was going, gone too fast.

This is the day I was reborn from a tragic death and the precarious pieces of a broken heart.

Light lends us the capacity of vision should we choose to open our eyes and see the beauty of color and shape of the soul.

3:00 a.m.

3:00 a.m. calls a tug-of-war
between dream and reality.
Eyes engage in battle—a left-right urgency.

Helpless churning belly
gulps a heartbeat—*defeated*.

The laptop now lights the quiet of darkest night.

Coffee brews.
First sip saves me every time.
Fingers, into the Cheerio's box.
Douse the hunger of emotion.

Glasses perch at the bridge of my nose.
Studious. A quick detour to social media
distracts from …

About to pour the heart's content,
so shaken from its sleep, onto a blank document.
Bring it to life with the death of so many things.

Hope it saves me like the pike roast.

Midnight Ramble

Help. God, help me, please.
The pain is a branding iron.
My heart bears the imprint:

A life that was everything—
all its imperfection, a solid foundation,
the consistent, dependable years.

I stir, gasp, and come alive in the mysterious hours,
3 a.m. acknowledging. Sheets of despair release
from the clamminess of skin rioting.

I cannot trust my memory playing tricks—
if ever it was sweet as the return rigorously portrayed
or a well-meaning intentional dementia.

I have tried earnestly to travel back in time,
to undo and reincarnate by bravery.

You call in a voice of now a time of bitterness—
the death of salvation.

Yes, it was all those things.
We know. And the betrayal is yours and mine
to own and bury with regret. Sleep,
only momentary, does not excuse or absolve.

Life. The daily minutia travels through us,
has no life in it at all. Fairytales.
Once-upon-a-time hope
wishes for death, its revival of jubilation.

Insomnia Law

Let it be law:

When insomnia strikes,
and worry-demons are at their best,
the bird's sunrise song goes quiet.

Great darkness engulfs their beaks.
The cheery wisdom can be death,
and the sun be overcome with gloom.

A chance that beauty may catch her rest.

So wickedly
dawn can have another day.

Road to You

Where does it lead from here?
A question the road directs to my feet.
Standing. Stomping. Still.
In a quandary, my toes and heels ponder.
How could it be the road not knowing
where it ends and where it goes?
I've become dependent, expecting that much.

Still, the road has no choice paved in permanency.
The twists and turns of gravel
are merely illusion in love with the soul in my feet.
They decide which way to go—free to choose.

And with all the power she asks the road,
"Carry me, please, on your back?
I'm afraid of direction, you see."

I will pirouette in position. Fall in love.
Give in to faith that wherever my feet are,
I am—if not anywhere, myself the way.

It is possible you can do everything and more impossible you can undo anything.

Every Day Since Then

Every day since then, you've died in small pieces,
fragments of you, disconnected, unaccountable,
gone astray—painful pockets in time, volcanic eruptions.
The formation of gems—a rarity
of perfection luminous among coal.
A cat's narrow eye, panoramic view, through
a lover's memory and a day gone by.

Every day since then, I've been at your impenetrable side
alone, trying to put the pieces of myself,
living inside of you, together.

Yesterday, tomorrow, today, every day since then …
a promise for a fully alive existence
outside of your shadow.

Love's Closet

It's just a dress.
   The louvered white doors slide left. Right.
   I close them and my eyes to the view.
   In there is a dance. Dinner. Lover. Smile.
   Dream. Perfect day. Scripture of the moon.
   How it was—went.
   The wind and tide spectacular and fleeting—
   I love you … I love you …

Dark flirtatious-haired woman—
   The other side safely detached.
   Sensuality zipped up, by choice wisely oblivious.
   Chocolate confessions and salted secrets.
   In a pound, two, ten … memories
   along with her size decline.
   So long.

The shuffle of wood hangers—
   Once a harp—eloquent—to the strumming of her fingers.
   A sentimental tune emerged surely remembering:
   Pink chiffon. The playful girl. White linen crisp on tan.
   Blue, yellow, green cotton laughter.
   Lavender nurturing, believing.
   Black lace sophistication! Red satin seductress!
   Die the death of love.

Wavering confidence in the mirror—
    Dare try on a pair of favorite heels. Taller.
    Dance in the silence of an abandoned room.
    Wish to walk under a glimmering night sky
    hand in hand, his voice landing softly like heaven.

Tears—
    Once beautiful pearls—a broken strand down cheekbones.
    Take a picture of yesterday, that day.
    She was … was …
    Too painful to forget.

Close the door—
    Heart in a hatbox.

Life has become a balance between mourning, the creative flow that it brings, and playful living when the sun shines once again.

Pieces

Everyone knows. Been here and there
in the dew of an innocent morning
or the wake of a bluish-gray sky. Seen what has passed
in the solitude of night. And Monday, well,
always gives way to Tuesday.

Still, not everyone remembers, nor do they intuit.
Everything, though different, is the same.
The heart tells a story; dreams remind me.

Regardless, someone will claim there's nothing,
make you question and give it away—an illusion.
They believe it will save the world and them.
Easier forgetting ...

But the background music—a twelve-note composition—
forever plays our emotional tones. And all eyes,
opened or closed, must recognize
dying to live again. One spectacular moment.

The only practical sanity: hope that you are
broken colored pieces, a kaleidoscope
about to form a butterfly.

Let us marry on Halloween and mask our selves in a costume of love.

A Bird

Today you are a bird. Pheasant. Ornately feathered.
The thin and broken smile has disappeared,
replaced by a pointed beak. It knows.
The tree's sturdy branches are your home.
The wind, while it blows furiously or settles calmly,
is an intimate friend. Call on her graceful magic.
Ease into the gap.
    No time.
        No death.
         No broken heart.
Everything found is free, and crumbs they are
so satisfying. Thank you! On a limb and in heaven
the air is ours to breathe in consummation.
Nesting.
    Searching worms.
        Lullabies.
Set our cares on fire. Release them and
the world to an underground prison.
    Fly free—
        simply don't trust landing!

Life promises magnificence if we accept not being truly attached to it, merely visitors in time and space, as educators of each other and students of God. We own nothing.

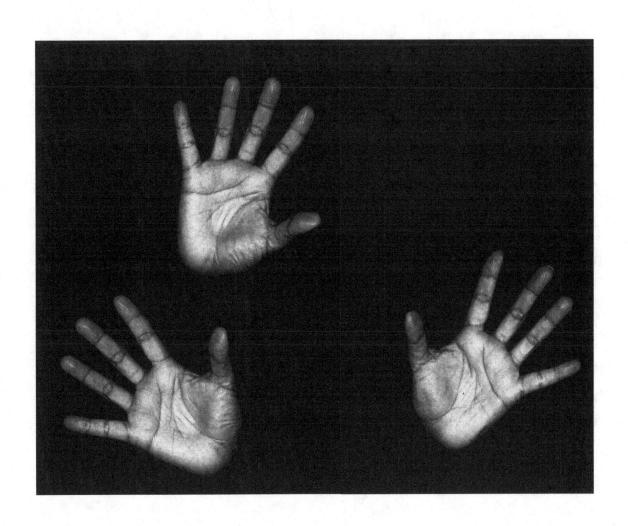

Song

The morning arrives late
and evening early.

All the in-between time.

Countless efforts,
vision and space blurred.
The maintenance of hope
to carry her delicately.

Fragments to a solution
lose me.

A windmill.
A viola.
A song in the wind.

Only the sea and one-eyed gull
understand.

Remember

Life's meaning
is love. The precarious
witch. The bastard for which
everything does and
does not make sense.
A wedding dance. Oh cliché,
gamble the house away!
Touch tender the spot,
what stings irrevocably
comes, or goes on and on,
like stars, their romanticized
version of the sky.
Tulips catch Sunday
afternoon's sunshine—
a well-dressed predicament!
We live and die pleading
for its capture.

Render our hearts helpless.

Manufacturing Ideas

On the outskirts of my mind
a wonderful idea is brewing,
stirring my curiosity.

Adrenaline hums within each cell. Fever.
The idea of "It" becoming tangible.

Feel the commotion attempting
to give birth to—
Giddiness grasps my will.
A panic ensues as to how or not.

I must travel across the horizon
of my thoughts, that tricky terrain,
to capture the magnificence

or close my eyes

and dream of brilliance.

Photograph by Maria Pisciotta-DellaPorte

Brilliant Orchestrators

They come like stars. See them there
in the thousands. Limitless discoverers.
Multiplying about love, angst, contentment.

Of all things, today, a pink cherry orchard:
You walking there in denim,
composing your thoughts.

It is unnecessary to understand, though
sometimes I do see it
like the green in your eyes.
Transcribe in poetic language
their message—little orbs
residing in pupils.

It's the song I hear. Without hesitation,
sing *Bel Canto.* Carry the weight momentarily
then disburse helium into vast pools
of universe. Collective energy.

A studio embraces me listening for miracles.
The sun through slanted blinds is a carpenter.
Brilliant hands designing Monets, Picassos
on an otherwise overlooked oak floor.

You! In Milan, Toronto, India,
Israel, Kansas, Belize. Unique as imagination.
Identical by a thread.

All of us human particles in a memory bank,
preserving for the future.
World in a nutshell.

God's Blue Eyes

At 2:00 a.m. I stir between the firm bed,
my permanent hip imprint on one side
and a cotton white sheet.

There is a sense of movement outside of myself.
The room with varying shadows cast from a light
on a cable box and the post office window.

Two slats of wooden blinds are caught open.
I look to see what I believe is a man, blue eyes
staring in at me. We communicate via telepathy:

What about me do you find so interesting?
Are you a gentleman? A sailor?
A villain or a spy?

"I trust I am a star."

If I count them in the sky, can I help you
get back to where you came from?

"You may. Only don't count yourself so lucky."
Oh please, I am not so naive!

Suddenly the blinds disappear.
Shadows become wings.
Light—a darkness giving way to perfect vision.
I am no longer in my bed but the hand of God.

The eyes of a man—a majestic ship carrying us,
two seagulls weightless upon the waves.
To the outer parts of the universe we go,
but not so far as to reach heaven.

Once again I find myself on my pillow,
wondering about things only earth can bring:
housekeeping, finance, relationships …
I should have known better than to dream.

The sailor at my window collected the ocean
in his eyes, all the wisdom of the galaxies,
and caught a passing cloud to Jupiter.

Who are we to say or question? This is borrowed time.
In fact, it may all be illusion.

Sole Warrior Soul

Purple has never been blind nor
a bird's song ever been deaf.

Those that are by choice and heart
will not conceive your struggle
to make visible the rainbow
or a chorus in the sky.

Best efforts will be beads of water
down the drain, never quenching thirst.

Grieve for a fleeting moment, I tell you,
then kiss it good-bye—a blessing.

Revel in the awareness rather than agonize.
Shift energy. No regrets but gratitude for
each joy and agonizing step that
built a champion heart,
sole warrior's soul.

One Piece Your Life

The ornamented box from which you were born—
a puzzle of five thousand and one pieces—
parents the corners that support
all the edges in your dreams.

Female and male connections:
piece them together—relationships.
Count the experiences—scattered planets
waiting to be discovered. As they unite,
build landscapes. Magnolia children.

Every part created brilliantly.
First love: a walk with Daddy and a lime lollipop.
A poem: Mother's beautifully creased hands nurturing.
Laughter: friends.
Competition, camaraderie, and loyalty: siblings.
Sacrifice: family.
Discovery, joy, wonder, and worry: a daughter.
Hope: marriage.
Pain: untimely death.

The seasons grew you sturdy, individual,
and as a joint part. So it goes.
The one extra piece is your search,
for from where you've come
there is a purpose.

Death Is a Song

Death is a song ever changing.
Time. Universal existence. Not
nailed down in a pine permanency.

The grave's an illusion. Conspiracy.
Its floating energy emerges around our hearts.
It's the life in between

all the things we've built—
relationships, broken promises, children—
that dictate the lyrics, define our purpose,
what we become by the road we lead.

Those that go on suffer the dying.
They cry, "Once love had a breath."
Brave soldier memories stick to their bones.
"Hover a moment," they ask, "to save us."

All the corpses in sorrow and retrospect.

In the end, we fight for our last breath rather than ease into it, not because we fear the unknown, pain, or what we perceive as death, but because we are saddened to go, to be alone, to no longer be a part of love, of the relationships we shared. For no matter how much suffering there ever was, it is glorious to realize we were part of something more extraordinary than ourselves. It is then that this knowledge—lost in time and search—rearranges what already flowed and will be realized, clear as day.

Rut

No more stuck-in-a-rut time.
It does not behoove you, by choice
or design, to give up, hover in the golden
waves of reprieve—the prisons of guilt and
survival imploding through awareness.

You cloaked yourself in a deafening silence
too long. Let the scars emerge proud,
mirrors into the soul. Toss the camouflage;
bully its thrusting trail from the past. Go,
a cheetah to a gazelle. Devour the future!

When the tears fall—and they will—
recall the many times you've risen
triumphant through their weight.

No refuge from life but a belly filled
with grief and joy.

Scattered feelings

I've no inclination to write a story.
Not today.

The day feels more like scattered feelings,
everything moving in the gray mist, searching
hopeful shadows of green satisfaction.

Escape into a moment. The world opens
her arms—an angel lover.

All doubt transforms to a mighty harvest,
glorious succulence.

There will be a covenant and
I shall abide in peaceful satisfaction.

Not in the fields of memory or the world
without love or you.

free

All I have is an empire built on love.
The palace—my heart—a cliché.
The care you would receive,
I would revel within, to share,
and so risk all my wealth:
a tentative welcome sign.

I've learned, you see, acrimoniously,
what one could steal unabashedly.

Yet every innocence is sincere.
It is possible to be pure in thought,
for the coveting …

A prize of naivety for a sinister thief.
Consequently, I give it away—

free, tenderly beating.

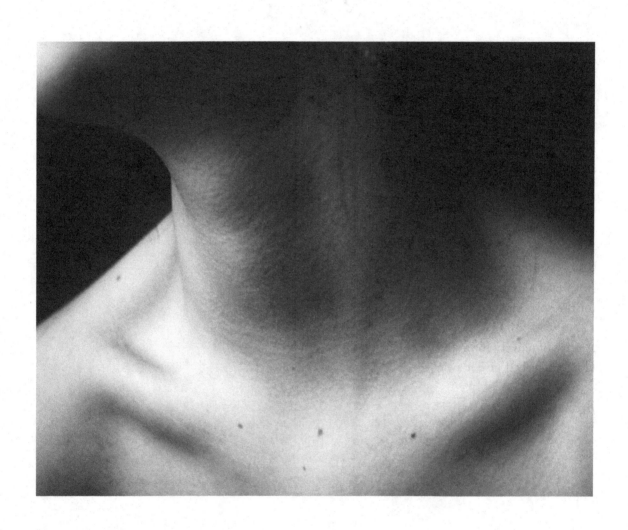

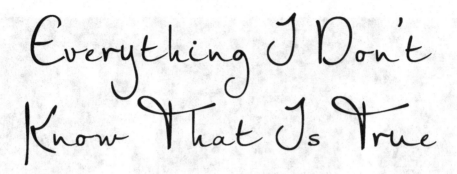

Everything I Don't Know That Is True

An unfortunate event occurred.
Somehow I disconnected
                         from a vaster intelligence.
Left here of earthly things,
            an extrasensory being—
And unless you are in love
     with yourself
       the world at your door
              is a curse!

Subconscious level grieves.
Knowing soul gathers
in my gut.
               Life—a place I struggle.
Wiser internal structure

        unwilling to adapt.

My mind is not always the most comfortable space.

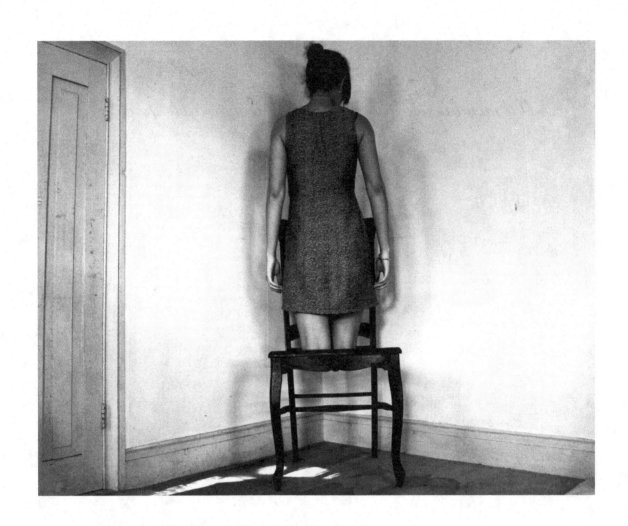

Swing High

When I was a little girl, I swung high and low,
tried to touch the clouds with my toes.
A pair of sneakers with worn-out laces
collected memories in dirt-filled soles.

Mill Pond: the trees I climbed,
each winding branch an invitation to soar
to new heights in the world and my spirit.

Days of tall grass fields, onion-scented and
honeysuckle sweetness.
Oh, the sun shone loudly—
a chorus in the sky!

Friends challenged one another
to balance, to walk on the white wooden fences
dividing us from the street and constructed belief.
I learned to stand tall on one leg,
the other behind, arms like a bird.

The breeze was delicate, innocence,
could carry you anywhere.

Sometimes with a close friend you'd simply
sit in wonder, talk secrets, collect ladybugs
that crawled onto summer-drenched skin.

We had no doubts. Honored our word.
Believed in the impossible.

Aged eyes see not so playfully
and not necessarily truth but fearfully.

Someone explains, "You can't …"
and being so smart you trust,
settle into the misfortune of doubt.

My little girl's heart is alive, in love, creating,
everything that I am.

She calls for me often to touch the sky with my toes,
even if it seems no one ever has or will.
"Be the one that tries rather than a hopeless fool!"
For rigid is the road to devastation.

You may toss your sneakers
and live your days in shattered bones.

When others imply to me, "You must have seen this coming," I want to assure them of my aptitude for enthralling denial.

In Light of the New Year

It's 2013, '14, '28. Yesterday was 1857, 1942, '79, '95.
Someone of importance was born to change the world
while others died alone, old, aching, insignificant.

    The young always discover.
    An event changed the course of life.
    Everyone broke someone's heart.

Your grandmother was there. My father too!
Washington, Martin Luther, John Lennon,
Mother Teresa, and Jesus. They built us.
Hitler, Stalin, Genghis Khan tried to destroy us.

    Yet the moon went down over the sea.
    The sun rose again over the mountains.
    As it ever shall be, world without end.

Here in New York and New Delhi, in Asia, Spain,
Turkey, Norway, Jerusalem, and Italy.
These places we call home:

Fragments of earth belonging to the stars
return to dust all of us, our blood a map of space.

In the palm of one another's hands—the waves of consciousness.
I will meet you there—a bell breaking the silence.
Promise you'll reach out and pull me from the unknown,
reintroduce me to your heart, my home.

In time we will be cast into the light,
once more perfect and innocent,
to become ourselves a cosmic truth.
Hold me delicately, as I you,
my universal soul.

When any human is purposely neglectful or cruel, not adhering to a moral code of ethics, it destroys all of us. We become the suffering bits and pieces of broken humanity.

faith

All the questions that answer "Why?"
I ponder, feeling guilty trying to understand
what perhaps I should simply accept.
Faith: learn the art to surviving madness.
Somehow, subconsciously trust
everything is perfect.

Worst-case scenario,
"happy-go-lucky" hasn't got your back.
You're thrown into a hellish assortment,
the dirtiest of shit.

"God," you ask, "Why do you patronize?"

Yes, I am bitter at this now.
Today I grew older by a lifetime—
Dreamt about floating in space, as if
I'd been there before. Remarkably dark
and vociferous. It frightened me to think
I could be there forever.

When suddenly nature, that feminine light,
shines in like a whore, legs wide open,
and screams, "You can!"
So I jump into love and look for you there.
Oh please ... And it could be laughter I hear
in response, or the wind. Either way,
in that second I am free.

Life Should Be

I left the city and its intellect—
the way it runs instinctively.
Steel and mortar adapt nature.
Traffic lights. Uptown, downtown,
west and east side. Yellow cabs.
The E, the F, the R …

Rushing corporate hounds.
Fancy offices, luncheons, holiday parties.
Politics. Law. Management. Headaches.
Overtime. Oh, the goddamn cash in it all!

I envisioned peacefulness. Live a simpler life
by the ocean, her waves telling not of stocks
and bonds or 401ks, but of nature.
Ride the tails of a dream. Begin well-intentioned.

You shrink to your family's needs. A fixture.
Voice less important.
Everything inside you shakes.
Where you've been and what you've learned
and become know better!

Still you give up your waist to the pain,
watch your regretful fingers feed your face numb.
Betray yourself again and again. Give way
to a cursed detriment. Fear you've forgotten.

Submitted to your husband's needs,
dreams, wants … wither, the consequence.
All your dancing pastels absorbed into a black,
egotistic heart.

The matriarch, nurturing, feeding, building the lives
of others. Unsung. Wind knocked out of breasts
by disrespect.

The home was love. Everything lay in its path:
meals, fabric, flowers, healing, tenderness …
all she ever wanted.

I contemplated an easier life. Eyes young
with enthusiasm. Hands soft and brilliant.
Life between grew weary, with its many deaths.
Taught me to dream about living.

When it comes to people, relationships, love, the heart knows. Even if it defies logic, love knows where it belongs. There is no compromise. If it works or not, there's a reason—right either way.

Bride to Desolation

The motion of words unspoken …
A bride to desolation—

Aged eyes beneath a veil of tulle
drift vacant, seek fulfillment,
a resurrected groom.

Bedroom reflections:
Chantilly Lace—
a floral heaven
in dormant space.

Disfigured heart.
The transition, a cancer,
quiet, cruel, and unforgiving—

Love everlasting.
La magnificent cliché.

Mocking Sun

The daytime cruelly mocks with its sun,
through every crevice a beam
of summer Creamsicle spun.

Cascading waterfalls on drapery
summon birds and their exuberant song.

Reflections: *another dimension*
from a gold mirror
casts shadow tribal dancers.

Listen for the echo down hallways,
a boy's deer-hide drum.

Perfect blooms of azalea multicolor smiles
fill up on moistened soil's energy.

An innocent glass perfume holder,
sitting blue upon a vanity, becomes a
kaleidoscope encouraging diamond-shaped
enthusiasm on an otherwise perfectly
content and empty wall.
Why does it not know beauty is strained
and the crows have left their markings.
Hope is out the window—
a neighbor whistling, dropping seeds
for grass to grow.

The day should remain indifferent.
Tomorrow can seize possibilities.

But the forecast calls for rain.

One innocuous day, evil came into the atmosphere and stole everyone's identity. I wept at the misfortune, thought what might I do, and then realized I never liked them much for who they were in the first place.

The Space Between

Between now and then, I often find myself—
dwelling in that weighty space,
a fluttering butterfly careful about
the perfect landing.

Glorious in-between time—
a sweet, refreshing breath, reprieve ...

About to embark upon a flower's gratifying nectar
then remembering—
             in love—
the damage it can cause.

A thorny rose bush on delicate wings—
take flight!

Counting His Demons

Together we sat counting his demons like crayons from a box.
So many colorful versions of the soul
up against the wall: Jim, George, Nathaniel …
Prepare for execution!

Shadows of himself cast against the innocence of dawning light,
a stable beige wall, a bipolar, schizophrenic fiasco.
I hate you!

I swear, this time he was sincere.
6:33 a.m. Yesterday's unmade bed, cold sweats,
sheets that stink of melodrama welcomed him
to hide from a now nearly sober state.
I lock him in,

prop a pillow at his spine. The good boy he once was
thanks me. Poor man. Gambler. Cheat. Brute.
What have they done to you?

Yes, my love, I know …
This is your dead father's gift. Remnants of his soul,
mightily waging war within you. Let us curse him wickedly,
though please do not abuse him in this your own haggard body.
And of course, it's entirely your mother's fault for leaving.
Damn her cancer!

When you awaken and the day seems forgiving,
I will make you oatmeal with cinnamon and cream,
nurture myself in normalcy.

Whistle and pretend
until one of your ghosts stabs me in the back.

My heart is my finest attribute and most difficult obstacle.

Rain

The rain is in rhythm. Heavy, full,
fat droplets by the million
intently release a flooded burden
feverishly to the ground,
momentarily savored before confiding
in rivers, merging into oceans.
Drink her purpose: to feed mighty earth,
grow his scent in colorful flowers.

A queen without a crown.

Every drop is an individual story; I listen
for answers in the empty space, between her stream,
learn as I watch gray dullness emerge into truthful
silver sparkle, my heart stilled.

Rain is a woman in love pouring out her heart.

When you're really quiet, people listen.

In the Land

In the land
    grass-blade kings dance
    fingers to a beat
    picking up the wind.
    Snow pollen melodies.
Summer
    restores easy thought.
    A rocking chair on the porch,
    its slow methodical meeting
    with a loose board, yawning.
Oak men
    with sturdy branches,
    their leaves of feminine delight.
    Bees understanding nectar's
    sweetness, gracefully
    balance the seasons.
The sky,
    infinitely blessed, holds her
    star jewels and lover, the moon.
Nature's heart
    cascades upon mountains
    into love she falls,
    water to her streams.

I wish for control over my mind when it comes to my heart, but in fact my heart has a mind of its own that seldom behaves.

Laura

Here I am—flowing microcosmic energy.

    Everything you *almost* see and feel,
    unwittingly.

Your mother first captured it for you:
A blue sky and floral ensemble.

Your father in the wind, surrounding.

Tenderness brought you here,
in fields of blazing stars. The grass roots
playfully encouraging your wonder.

Discover:

If the day and its sunshine could sing,
what would it, for you?

    Love, let it be love.
    I do…

In a world so forgetful,
    be the air

though unrecognized, faithfully
everything in life.

Photograph by Maria Pisciotta-DellaPorte

Shadow Mood

Shadows
    down the hallway
    through vine and fruit
    curtains—not my style.
    The onset of a storm—
    a tucked-in mood.

Cotton fleece throw
    away from life's defeating days
    the ones that grow you old,
    harshly aware of
    and away from
    innocence.

Today
    summons simplicity.
    A black-and-white spotted dog
    wags his tail for a bone.
    Canned soup from the pantry—
    warm and soothing lentil.

An Italian landlady
    has home-baked bread
    freshly wrapped for sharing.
    Salted butter will melt into crevices,
    bliss on the tongue.

Quiet
    except for pipes clink-clanking
    heat through the baseboards.

Safe haven
    repairing,
    preparing.

Hope on the doorstep
    is like milk and sunshine.
    Tomorrow is another day.

It takes a little bit of everything.

The Pancake

I'd like to bid farewell to fifteen pounds,
the nostalgic pancake that I am,
but, oh, how bittersweet their memory.

The griddle sizzles.
Little water bubbles spritzed from my fingertips
hop about, hot, in joyfulness.
    It is a Saturday past, long past—

The sun is shining a 1970s toss
between innocence and change,
a brightness unscathed by disappointment
and a thousand types of death.

My mother's apron is colorful fruit,
a vine of commitment tied with certainty
around a waist expanded and retracted,
seven times giving life.

Butter's sweetness fills the air.
A table adorned in triangle folded napkins,
orange juice glasses with floral stems.
Maple's woody-amber flavor drizzles
swirls with all the answers.

My father's seat most prominent
at the head of the table.
He serves and is served respect.

Buckwheat, vanilla, eggs, and milk—
a batter churned and flipped golden-brown.

Sisters enter, each with their own style:
hippie, humble, tough, dreamer, conceited,
blue eye shadow.

Brothers are dark-haired princes.
Protectors. Adventurers. Learners.
Sometimes pleading for no sisters.

An AM/FM radio sits sturdily on a
Formica kitchen counter, plays mellow rock,
matches the mood of a Long Island breeze
swaying gently the sheer-white curtains,
a lilac scent on their tail.

A dog named Pinky sits on a window seat,
watching for bicyclists. Sets off her beagle's bark.
Soon to be indulged with scraps.

Oh, how I love a good pancake: sweetness of life
stacked, circle of heaven cut into
and delightfully consumed.
Satisfy a space for peace, happiness,
and hope.

What once was … in every bite.

Photograph by Maria Pisciotta-DellaPorte

Do Not Disturb

There are fifteen pounds of solid protection handy in the pantry.
It screams from a maddening silence: Do not intrude!
Tired. Afraid. Guilty. Insecure. *Unavailable.*

A moment, please,
to work on myself ...

The purpose it serves is worthy.
I am—
of the peace.
Still, not with a banner please,
to the world a double chin.

I've been somewhere frightened, hurt,
met the challenge.

A map to my soul,
words and wounds.

Ask that the world read my body:
a story of bravery not weakness.
Afford the space—haven—
to claw your way back ...
fingers to the bone.

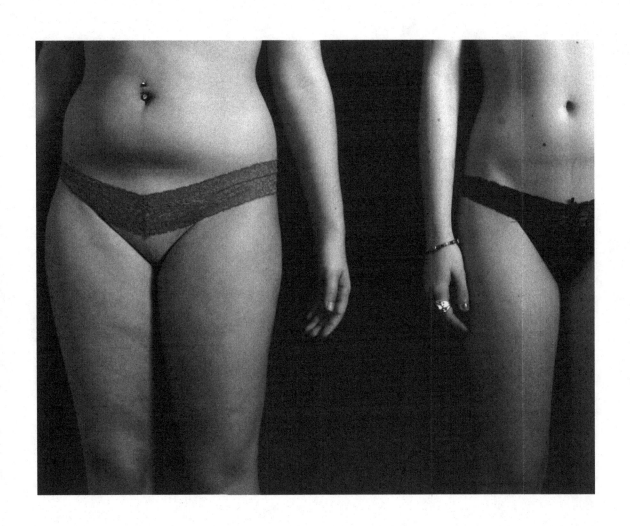

You couldn't catch the moon chasing kittens, as if you could ever catch the moon.

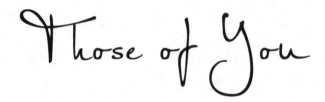

Those of You

I am in the midst of love—
always, unwittingly, purposefully,
moments into year after year,
encapsulated by love.

In the soul of a recipe—a great aunt's,
grandmother's—
preserved in a worn tin canister
that would tell stories if it could,

old tying into the new:
a mother's aging hands teach
about kneading.

What we value
essentially is who we become.
I am you, forever.

When I recall your heart, there is my own.

And though voices in memory may be
too distant to capture, I allow the shadows
of your smiles to cloak me in the warmth
of perfection—how it feels to have known you.

A day in which the intimacy of life escaped,
I was reborn with you in recollection
because you were and I am.

Photograph by Maria Pisciotta-DellaPorte

The Breaks

Our moments of brief affections seemed timeless,
always were all that they promised to be—
in the breaks, the grueling hours between.
Their memory recalling, wanting
the fulfillment of what it aught to be
more than the tease of promise.

A thirst never quenched but wine on my lips,
hoping, gathering fragments of his energy—
a dull diamond dust's capacity to shine.

Come to terms with the emptiness of
where you almost were captured in
satisfaction. Waited too long.
Your search for the right answers
between mistresses' legs.

The precious romance of your traveling tongue
was perfection upon each of their erect nipples.

Came home one last time
to say, "I love you."

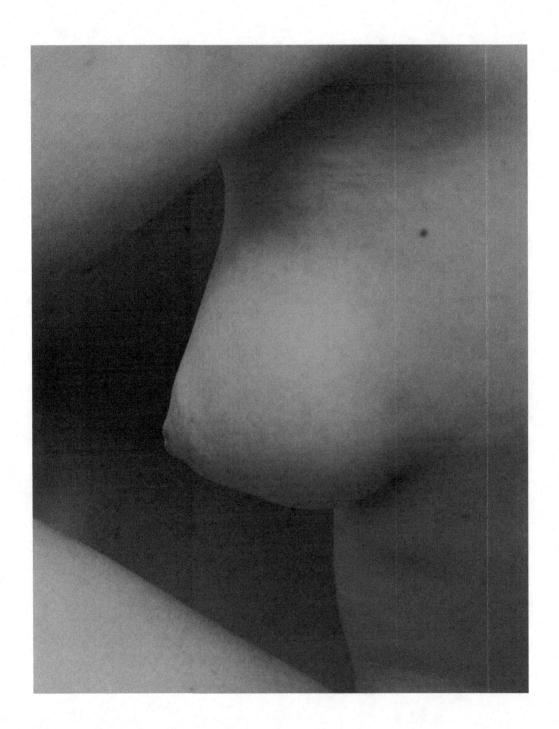

It is the days that try most to break you that make you.

Death

Death is a profound silence
heard painfully loud and clear.
A trumpet echoing energy

of the life gone from us,
its irreplaceable charisma.

Every movement is asleep,
crying of the moments that are
years of lackluster:
an ironing career, scrubbing the
crevices of a bathtub with a toothbrush.

A walk on an old road recalls the name,
a once-loved song gone melancholy.

Your hollow insides beg to implode,
learn how not to feel.
Cast prayers to the sky.

A sole leaf replies in whisper from
the breathless ground, "I'm sorry,"
as lilac's purple runs pale.

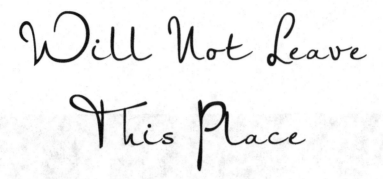

Will Not Leave This Place

Tell me, you have the mourning touch,
a magnetic sun for gathering pieces
into the light, a swirled peppermint in
your pocket ready for the offering.
Quench my dry tongue its bitterness,
will you?

Of course you remain hopeful, a brave
soldier sturdy on your feet, prepared
to carry the wounded, seared flesh back to
health. I will, however, not leave this space,
infested as it may be.

Days of gambling through secret entries
for an old biscuit or hardened cheese,
impractical. A dead mouse, I tell you.
The trap has snapped its scrawny neck!

Sell happily-ever-after to the politician.
She's ringing at your door for votes. I hear they're
giving out free pens with a save-the-world flyer.
You can etch your heart and mail it to the stars.

Steel Pink

A steel pink heart—
magnolia-scented wind.
Take notice of the evergreen,
her bouquets offering spring.

Walk in the lane, carefree spirit.
Greet her Southern charm.
It is good—

in the gentle breeze enraptured
by wisps of honey hair and a delicate silhouette.

Find yourself most willingly set free,
imprisoned simultaneously—
sensitively in her love.

for a Prince

Tonight is a song
I have yet to hear.

In fact, it is all I know
by memory, the truth …

Believe you are here
in my heart,
indeed singing.

By day and long years—

Remember
the church in your eyes,
faith I had in the melody
of your touch.

Have become a graceful swan
dancing on the water,
your lily-pond reflection.

Daydreaming

Mind out

in the fields:
a wildflower dance,
springtime,
honeysuckle breeze.

At sea:
adrift, salted air,
sunset orange-popsicle sky
releasing the moon.

Desert:
dry warmth
inviting waterfall mirage,
hula girls quenching thirst,
serving fruit in a coconut shell.

Not here!
Dull with work confinement,
but there …

on a breeze
and a song.

Bird

Inside, the bird there is a humming.
Rapid heart rate.
Skeleton. Fetus.
Outside, the wind blowing.

Between beams of light
and dark moon—birth.
A song. Cry. Whisper.
Miracles of the sky echoing
long distances to meet wherever
you are.

Ghosts collect their haunted pasts
and go. Another day without you.

Search for crumbs. Innocence.
A universe with no wings.

Need

I need time to float at ease,
to catch up before I dare to get ahead.

Fall apart remembering …
to forget again.
Rebirth … hope it catches me
on an upswing.

A bonfire for burning
memories, their essence.
Black smoke-ghosts swirling
twisters. Fire in your dreams.

Someone or other to understand.
If it all adds up …

Hope that some random moment,
we can grasp what was.

Smile subtly aware.

Hoodwinked

One day you wake up
instinctively, wanting to be a bird.

You grow feathers of prominent red,
streaks of bold black.

Your lips pucker and harden,
triangle themselves into a beak.

A tune from another world bellows
innately from your tiny ribcage.

Oh, and that hopeful fast-beating heart—
I believe ... I believe ...

Set off to fly!
The dream I was sold by angels.

Gaze downward disenchanted,
feet planted firmly on the ground.

The devil stole my talons
one digit at a time.

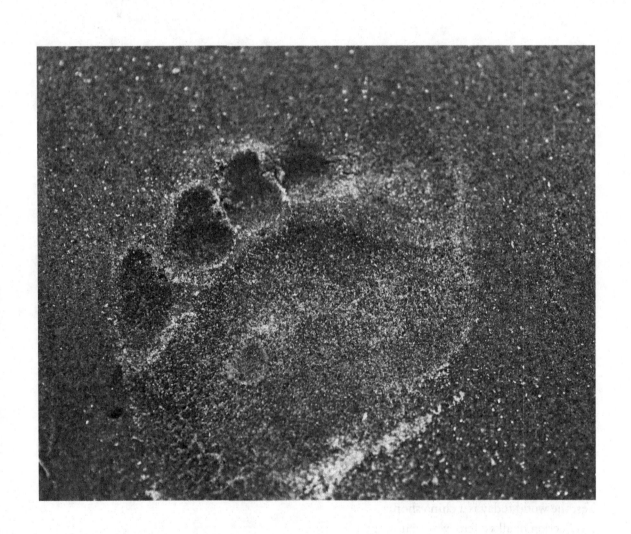

Without the Identifier

I've come back a feather spirit,
the weightiness of complication buried,
to collect who I was: the noble remains.

A cashew out of its poisonous shell.

Unsuspecting victim, I was myself the murderer.

The girl with a yellow hem slit her wrists
on a cantaloupe. Sticky fingers.

The tragedy didn't save anyone but
the monsters we forget.

The sun shines unexpectedly on a Monday.
Careful! Steady, even steps.
Everything is mysteriously lenient.

Ladylike,
the curtains, how they drape perfectly.
A female ghost's silhouette.

Yes, the world today is a china shop,
a collection of all yesterday's teacups:
vines, delicate rims, curved handles
for nuzzling a hooked finger.

The soft whispers that try to remind
you like sugar cubes. Each sip
the consequences killing sweetly.

Mine

This short space long in endurance
has an abundance of fragments to
pull apart and reassemble. Where once
there was a singular motion, belief,
awareness, and identity. *Perhaps
all illusion* ...

Oh, but it was a life; we had a road to follow!
A perfect wisdom.
Trust. Damn it all to hell!
The foundation was quicksand.

Honey, we've no more time.
Capture the remnants—sweet marmalade
on your tongue—then kiss me good morning.
Quickly! Before it all dissipates—a humid breeze.

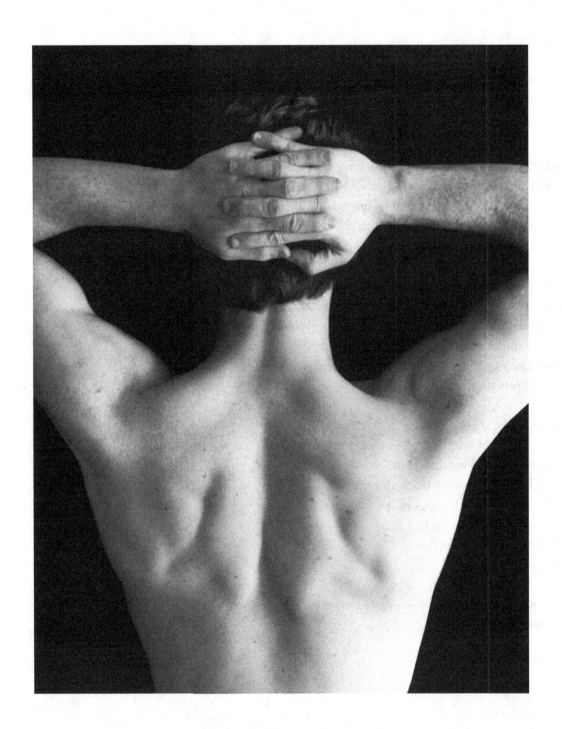

Admittedly

There's a shadow on my back watching, listening.
I feel compelled to answer to the son of a bitch.
Meanwhile, I don't want to be censored.
Why do I have to explain myself to you … you …
    and fuck him quite honestly!

I begin to retract my common sense, go all whiny
like a six-year-old, stepping up on my toes,
pushing my heels outward, pulling up on the hem
of my skirt, contorting my arms behind my head
with excuses! I hate the weakness. You just want
    to piss yourself.

Repress the anger. Fear and stuff it down,
a good dose of salty-sweet blood on your teeth.
Pretend. One, two, three, whoever you need to be safe.
You know there's only black and white.
It's shown its pearly fangs in the darkness,
unexpected around corners.
Better not to be right, but
    choose wisely.

Go mad searching—you—*a brave confession*
admittedly.

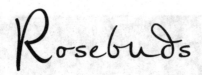

Rosebuds

Sadness bellows in every ice droplet
falling from the winter sky.
A gray solitude too bitter for the heart's survival.

Here in a room of yesterday,
all the distracted shadows on lonely walls
search a soul—the warmth of flesh—
and attach themselves to a story called love.

A promised future: recall gold and pink
painted propositions, diamond-cut fingers.

The expectancy gave way to death.
All life's highlights the dances of flourishing energy
transformed: harsh, jagged complications.

Circumstance conceals once-upon-a-time
sweetness doused like fire, down like poison.

She awoke among rosebuds, the prettiness
of a canvas backdrop,
herself a hollow silhouette.

A Penny Wish

Everybody with something to say …
I write my mind, not speaking so dangerously,
every thought choreographed, singular,
the moment gathering me up, giddy,
capricious, about to fall off the edge.
As I paint, each word dances on the page,
arms in flight a ballerina, *Adagio,*
grande jeteé—

Into that place I am free, *oh so young.*
Where I can choose my burdens?
Buttercup kisses heavy on my lips.

Exhale the proverbial punch in the heart.
Coming to terms … the way it shakes me.
I'd rather be a raindrop falling upward,
treble keys, high notes, on a piano.
Swirling dancer in a jewelry box.

Toss a penny and wish.

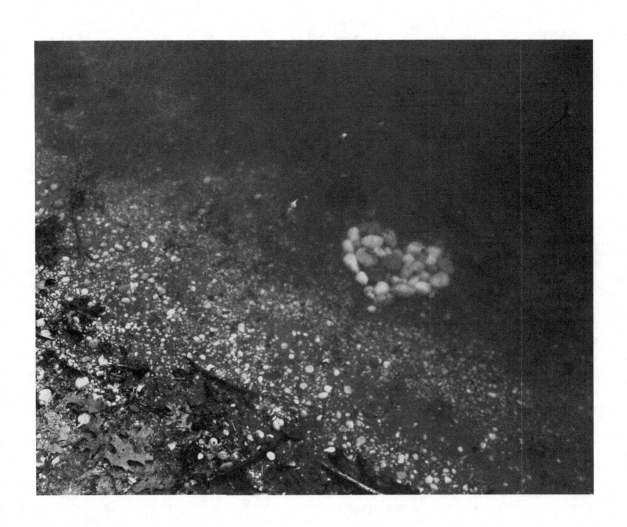

Wings

I wear my heart on my sleeve.
    I need longer sleeves.
They can become wings
    of pink cashmere
And lift on a breeze

Cinnamon-scented love beneath
miles into the atmosphere.
Above circumstance.

Find arms wide and cradling.
Let go—receive
    microgravity in my feet.

Never need land again.

Photograph by Maria Pisciotta-DellaPorte

Printed in the United States
By Bookmasters